SPACE TRAVEL

Roy Bentley

Macdonald Educational

How to use this book

First, look at the contents page opposite. Read the chapter list to see if it includes the subject you want. The list tells you what each page is about. You can then find the page with the information you need.

If you want to know about one particular thing, look it up in the index on page 31. For example, if you want to know about astronauts, the index tells you that there is something about them on pages 6 and 7. The index also lists the pictures in the book.

When you read this book, you will find some unusual words. The glossary on page 30 explains what they mean.

Series Editor
Margaret Conroy

Book Editor
Polly Dunnett

Series Design
Robert Mathias/Anne Isseyegh

Production
Marguerite Fenn

Picture Research
Suzanne Williams

Factual Adviser
Dr John Griffiths

Reading Consultant
Amy Gibbs

Teacher Panel
Stephen Harley
Ann Merriman
John Allen

Illustrations
Peter Bull 6–7, 24–25
Robert Burns 10–11, 12–13, 15, 17, 18, 28–29

Photographs
Courtesy Marconi: 21
NASA: 14, 16, 17, 19T, 20, 22, 23, 26–27
Space Frontiers/Daily Telegraph Colour Library: cover, 8–9, 19B, 27R, 28
Tass: 12
ZEFA: 8T

CONTENTS

PEOPLE IN SPACE

Living in space

Imagine yourself all wrapped up in your thickest clothes, ready for the worst weather. On Earth, your clothes would protect you. Out in space, they wouldn't help at all. You would be dead in less than a minute, because space is cold and empty. It has none of the things we need to live.

On Earth, we are surrounded by air, which we breathe to stay alive. Air is also quite heavy. The weight of the air above us is called pressure, and we can't survive without it. In space, there is no air, so astronauts have to stay inside cabins, or wear spacesuits, that hold air in and keep the pressure right.

In space, everything is weightless and floats around. This can be fun, but if astronauts stay weightless for too long, their bones and muscles become weak. They have to do special exercises to stay fit.

There are many other dangers in space. For example, there are bits of rock called meteoroids flying around. The air above Earth prevents most of these from reaching the ground. But the thin walls of a spacecraft can only stop the smallest meteoroid. Astronauts have to be very brave to travel in space.

An astronaut floating in space wears a body-shaped airtight bag – his spacesuit. He moves around by controlling small jets of gas that shoot out from his backpack.

The spacecraft in the picture is a space shuttle. The crew live and work in the small front area which also carries all the food, water and air the crew need. The larger area at the back is for cargo.

Earth is surrounded by a layer of air called the atmosphere. It gradually thins out, and space begins about 100 kilometres above Earth.

fuel tanks

flight
deck

cargo
bay door
closed

living and sleeping deck

atmosphere

robot arm

cargo bay door open

Destination Moon

Twelve astronauts have stood, walked, worked and slept on the Moon, 380 000 kilometres away. This is the furthest people have ever been away from Earth.

All the people who have been to the Moon so far have been American. It took the Americans ten years of planning to get them there. Before they could send people, they had to send robots, to see if spacecraft could land safely. They also sent spacecraft with cameras to take pictures of the best places to land. They built bigger and bigger rockets, to blast the spacecraft off on their long journey to the Moon. The biggest and most powerful rocket was called Saturn V.

Blast off for 3000 tonnes of metal and fuel. The Saturn V rocket is sending three astronauts to the Moon.

space car

At first, the Americans sent only one astronaut into space, then two. Finally, they sent the three astronauts who were the first people on the Moon in 1969. Their spacecraft was Apollo 11, and the part that landed was called the lunar module.

Other astronauts who landed later drove around the Moon in the first space car. They explored, did experiments and collected rocks for scientists back on Earth to study. They found that the Moon was an empty place, with no plants or animals.

The last mission, or journey, to the Moon was in 1972. There are no plans to send anyone back there just yet. But when people do go back, they will probably take bulldozers and explosives to dig for the Moon's metals.

Astronauts on the surface of the Moon. You can also see the lunar module and the space car.

lunar module

The space shuttle

A few minutes later, the fuel tank falls away.

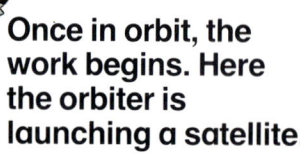

Once in orbit, the work begins. Here the orbiter is launching a satellite.

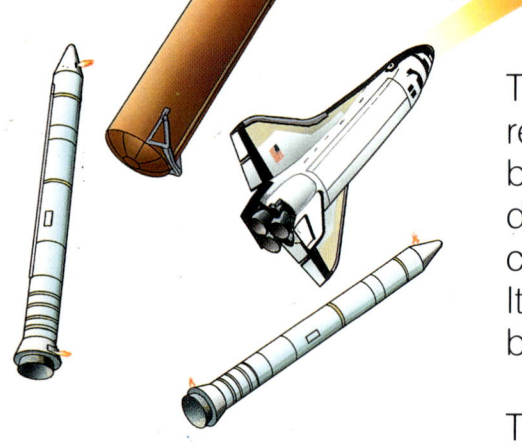

The Americans spent billions of dollars trying to reach the Moon, using spacecraft that were only built to last for one flight. Then their scientists designed a new kind of spacecraft that was cheaper to run. They called it the space shuttle. It saves money because most of its parts can be used over and over again.

The part of the shuttle that carries people and cargo is called the orbiter. Rocket motors and boosters send it into space, and it flies back to land like an ordinary aeroplane. The orbiter and rocket boosters can be used again. The only part that is lost each time is the fuel tank.

The shuttle has other advantages. For example, it has a very big cargo bay which is the place where things are carried or stored.

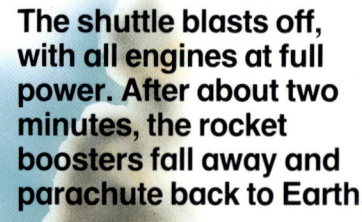

The shuttle blasts off, with all engines at full power. After about two minutes, the rocket boosters fall away and parachute back to Earth.

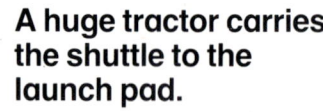

A huge tractor carries the shuttle to the launch pad.

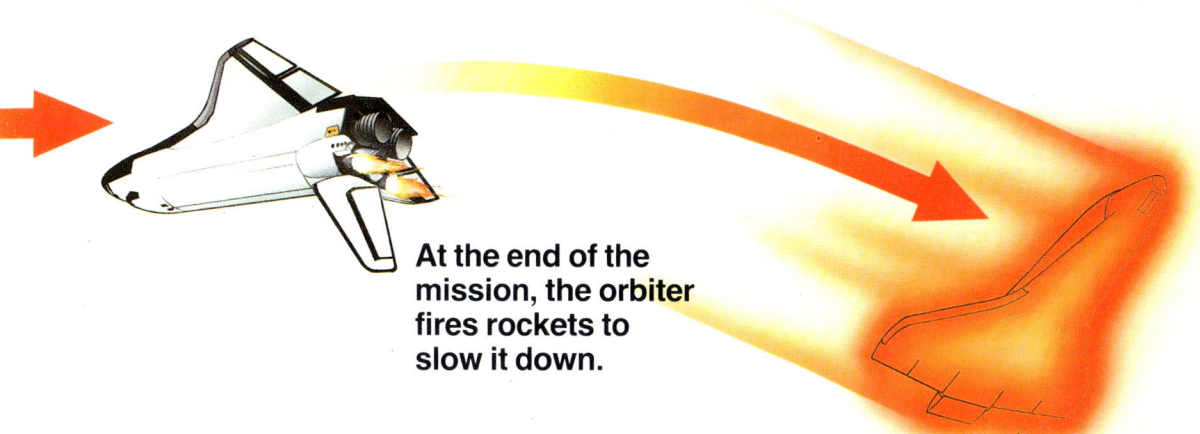

At the end of the mission, the orbiter fires rockets to slow it down.

The cargo bay can take things of all shapes and sizes, even other spacecraft.

Most spacecraft that carry people take off and land at very high speed, and astronauts need special training to be able to cope with the force of this. The shuttle takes off and lands more gently. People do not need to be trained like astronauts to fly in it. This means ordinary scientists can travel into space, so long as they are fit and healthy.

The shuttle doesn't save quite as much money as people hoped. One shuttle, called Challenger, exploded in 1986, which showed that space travel is still very dangerous. But in spite of these problems the shuttle programme will continue.

The orbiter turns over and glows red hot as it re-enters the atmosphere.

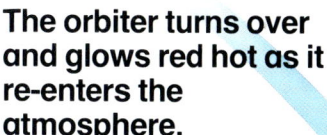

Coming in to land, the orbiter turns again and uses its wings to glide downwards.

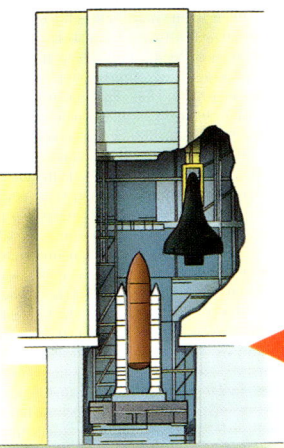

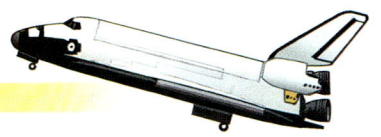

11

Space stations

We now know that people can travel through space. The next step is to build spacecraft that people can live in. These are called space stations.

Some people have already tried living in space. Between 1971 and 1981, the Russians sent up six space stations, all called Salyut. Crews of astronauts flew up and stayed in them for months. Smaller spacecraft brought them the food and other things they needed.

The Americans have launched one space station called Skylab. It was made from part of a leftover Moon rocket. It is still the biggest space station ever built. The cabin was as big as a two-bedroom house.

space shuttle

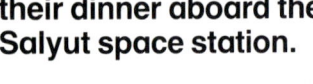

These Russian cosmonauts are having their dinner aboard the Salyut space station.

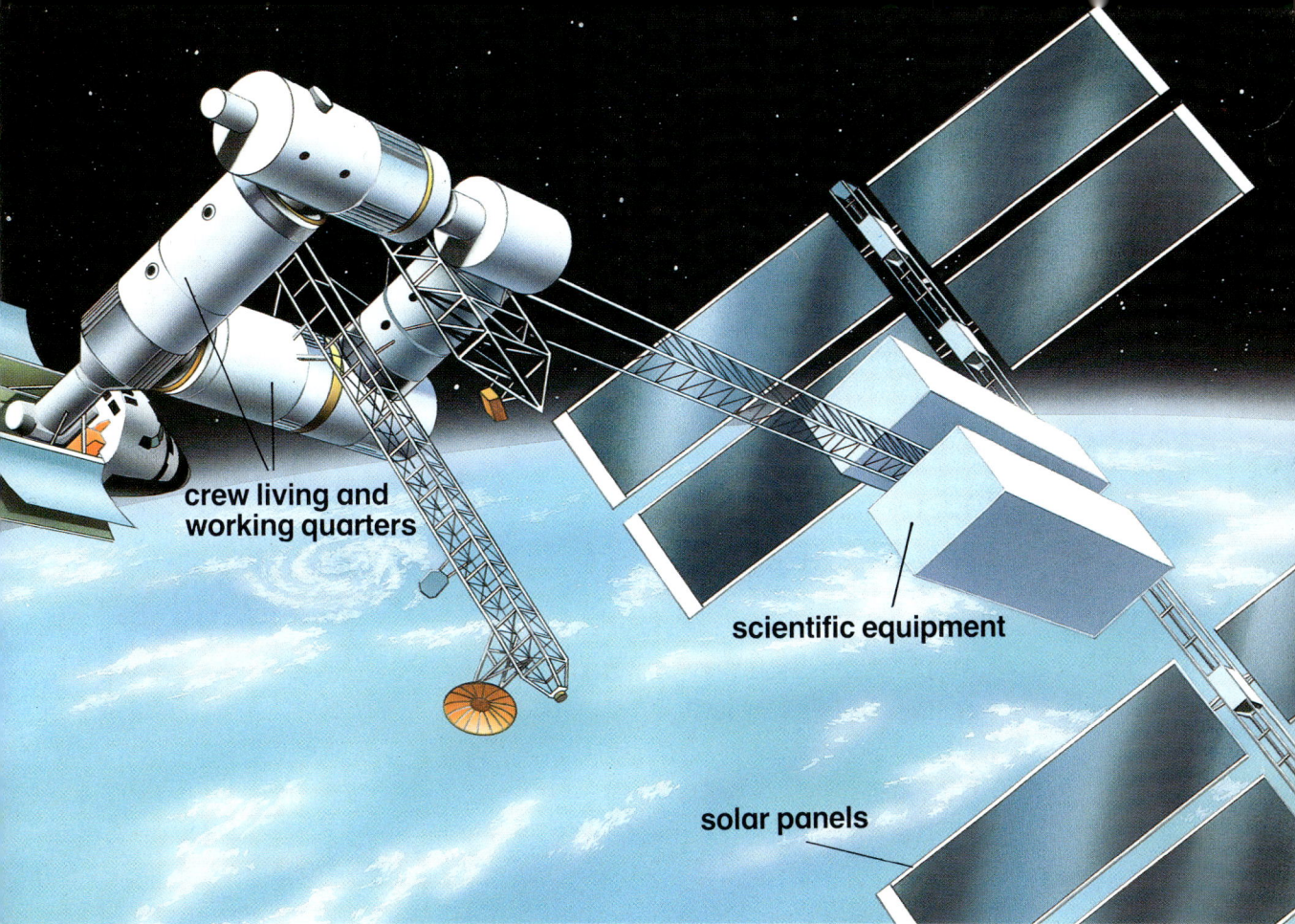

crew living and working quarters

scientific equipment

solar panels

All these stays in space have just been tests to find out how long people can live there, and how useful space stations really are.

Space stations will be places where certain drugs and metals can be made better and cheaper than on Earth. Some of these can only be made where there is no air. To make them on Earth, you have to build special rooms with no air in. Other drugs and metals can be made more easily in weightless conditions. It may be worth building space stations, so that drugs and metals can be made out in space, where everything is weightless and there is no air.

The Americans plan to build a new space station in the 1990s. This is how it may look. The space shuttle will carry it up in bits. The bits will then be fitted together in space. Space workers will live and work in the tube-shaped parts.

MACHINES IN SPACE

Earth satellites

Have you ever watched the weather forecast on television and seen the cloud pictures? Have you ever heard a news report from somewhere far away across the world? All these words and pictures have been sent to you through space, from a satellite.

Satellites travel round and round, or orbit, Earth. They are the most important kind of spacecraft but they have no people on board. There are hundreds of satellites up there in space, all of different shapes and sizes. Almost all are of two main kinds – 'watchers' and 'senders'.

The watchers have special cameras that send their pictures down to Earth. They photograph clouds, ice fields, storms and droughts. They can take pictures of fields and oceans to show how well crops are growing, or whether there are plenty of fish in the sea.

The senders are powerful machines that pick up radio signals and send them across the world. They send the pictures on your television screen, and information from one computer to another. If you have ever telephoned someone a long way away, a satellite may have sent your words thousands of kilometres through space.

A 'sender' satellite is prepared for launch.

Satellites in their orbits round Earth. Intelsat is a communications satellite, or 'sender'. Meteosat is a 'watcher'. It takes pictures of cloud formations to help scientists forecast the weather.

Meteosat

Intelsat

Robot landers

People have travelled only as far as the Moon, which is Earth's nearest neighbour in space. Machines have gone much further.

The Moon travels round and round Earth and Earth itself is one of nine planets that travel round and round the Sun. Some machines have landed on the nearest planets, which are Mars and Venus. The machines are called robot landers.

Robot landers usually have two parts, a 'mother' craft and a 'daughter' robot. The two travel through space joined together. A rocket in the mother craft keeps them on the right course, and when they reach the planet, the 'mother' launches them into the right path, or orbit, around it.

A close-up photograph of the rocky surface of Venus, taken by a Russian Venera lander.

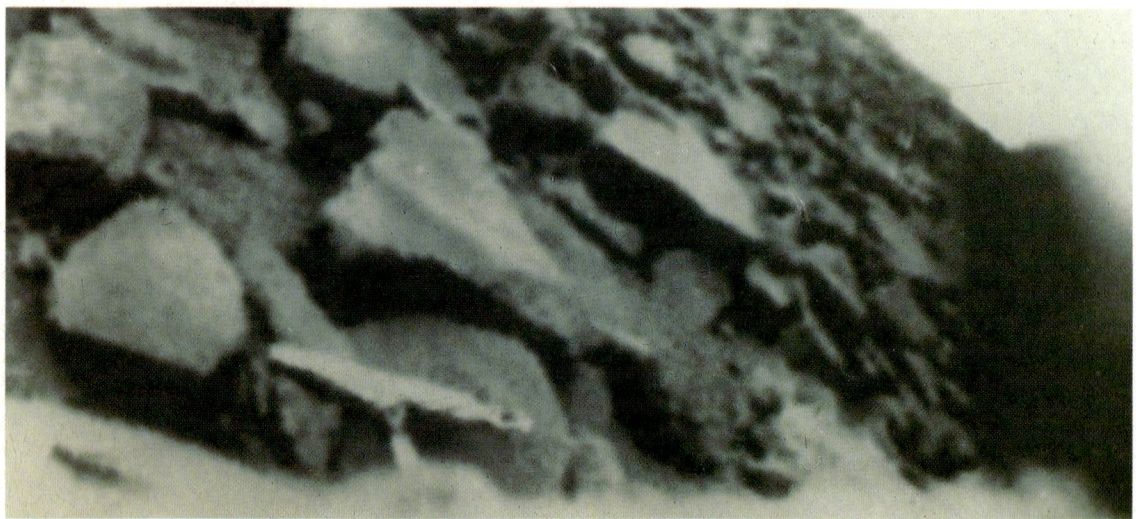

Then the mother and daughter separate. The mother craft stays in orbit and sends pictures and messages to Earth. The daughter lands and sends pictures to the mother.

The lander has a much more dangerous job to do than the mother craft. It travels very quickly through any gases that may be round a planet. This makes the lander very hot so it needs a shield to protect it from the heat. It also needs rockets or parachutes to help it land gently so that it does not get damaged. The planet it lands on may be burning hot or freezing cold, and the lander must be tough enough to stand up to this, too.

The Viking lander.

The American Viking lander took this picture of the red Martian desert. The lander found no signs of any life.

Deep space

Several spacecraft travel in deep space, far away from the warmth and light of the Sun. Some of these have passed the distant planets of Jupiter and Saturn. One is on its way to the stars, which are other suns, very much farther away from us than the planets that travel round our Sun. It will take eight million years for the first spacecraft to reach the stars.

Spacecraft that travel in deep space are similar to the 'watcher' type of satellite. They send pictures and other information back to Earth. They follow a very exact path between all the moons and planets they pass on their long journey. Sometimes they can even be made to change course.

The flight path of the Voyager 2 spacecraft. Starting from Earth, it passed the planets Jupiter, Saturn and Uranus. Now it is on its way to Neptune.

The swirling clouds of Jupiter, photographed by Voyager 2. You can see two of Jupiter's moons in front of the clouds.

The spacecraft that met Halley's Comet in 1986 also followed very accurate courses. Comets are balls of frozen gas and dust that travel in huge orbits. Halley's Comet only comes in near the Sun every 76 years. Scientists had to send off spacecraft months in advance to meet the comet before it returned to deep space.

Scientists have learnt a lot from these journeys into deep space. They now know that Jupiter is a colourful ball of gas, surrounded by a ring of deadly rays. Some of its moons are frozen balls of ice, while others have volcanoes that shoot rock and gas out into space.

Pictures of the planet Uranus were taken by Voyager 2 in January 1986. This photograph shows one of the moons of Uranus, called Miranda.

BEFORE LAUNCH

Planning a space mission

When a spacecraft takes off from the ground, it is the start of another journey into space. It is also the end of years of work on Earth. As the spacecraft's computers take control, the hundreds of people in mission control, and the thousands in the factories that made the spacecraft, can only watch and hope that everything goes well. And it all started with one idea – to build a spacecraft.

These astronauts are practising being weightless. They are in an aeroplane, where weightless conditions can be created for a few minutes at a time.

There is a lot of paperwork to do before a spacecraft can be built. This woman is working on the design. Computers and other modern technology are used at all stages.

But what should the spacecraft be like? First, engineers must work out what things the spacecraft will have to do. How far will it go, how long will it be in space, what will it carry? There are a million questions to answer, and a million things to design and make. It takes many hours on the computer to find all the answers, and many people to do all the work. It took twelve years of planning before the first space shuttle could be launched in 1981.

While the spacecraft is being planned and built, the astronauts are chosen and trained. They must be ready when the spacecraft is finished. Pilots practise flying the spacecraft. Others practise the work they will do in space. They often spend many hours in special swimming pools that make their bodies feel very light. Out in space, they will weigh nothing at all and they must know what it feels like.

Building a spacecraft

When the engineers have worked out what the spacecraft has to do, they can start designing it. The craft must be as light as possible. Then it will use less fuel and won't need such big, expensive rocket engines to launch it. It must also be strong enough to stand up to take off and landing.

If it is a robot lander craft, it may need legs to stand on. And the lander must be built to last in places very different from Earth.

Before the shuttle was built, many different designs were drawn, and some of these were made into test planes. This picture shows a test plane landing.

If it is going to fly through the Earth's air, or the air of another planet, the spacecraft must be streamlined. This means that its shape must be smooth and rounded so that it can glide more easily through the air. Out in space, there is no air to get in the way, so there spacecraft can be any shape.

Inside one of the world's biggest buildings, the shuttle orbiter, fuel tank and rocket boosters are fixed together.

The engineers must also think about the kind of power to use. Many spacecraft get their power from the Sun. They use the sunlight that always shines in space to make electricity.

Before choosing the best design, engineers try out many different models. Factories all over the world start making the parts, and then the parts are put together near the launch pad, where the craft will take off.

A SHUTTLE MISSION

Blast off

'Zero minus ten seconds and counting.' These are the words you hear just before lift off. You are the pilot of the space shuttle, strapped into your seat and looking up at the sky.

The engines start up. A voice shouts 'Zero!' and the booster rockets blaze into life. The locks holding the shuttle snap open, and the shuttle blasts off the ground. The power of the engine pushes you back into your seat.

Two minutes later, the booster rockets stop. With a flash, small rockets push them away from the shuttle and they parachute back to Earth. For another seven minutes you sit, pushed into your seat by the speed of the shuttle. Even your eyes feel heavy as they check the dials and instruments in front of you.

Suddenly you're weightless. The main engines stop and the empty fuel tank outside falls away. The small shuttle engines fire twice. You and the computers carefully control each engine to get the exact speed and distance from Earth that you want.

You have arrived in space. Your mission has started.

Capturing a satellite

One of the jobs you must do on this mission is to bring back a damaged satellite. To do this, you must get into your spacesuit. It takes two hours to put it on. You wear a suit that keeps air in, and special underwear to keep you cool inside it, as well as gloves, boots, helmet and jet-powered backpack.

Then you must sit for three hours, breathing in the special air that spacesuits are filled with. Five and a half hours after you started, the outer hatch swings open and you step out into space.

Getting a captured satellite into the cargo bay can be a difficult job. Here two astonauts are working together, without the help of the shuttle arm.

26

You see the satellite and the shuttle's long arm reaching towards it. With your rocket jets pushing you forward, you float away from the shuttle. You stop just two metres away.

Through the radio in your helmet, you talk to the person controlling the arm. You help him to line it up with the bolts on the satellite. Then you turn the bolts to lock the arm and the satellite together. Slowly the arm twists the satellite round and places it in the shuttle's cargo bay. You unlock the arm.

Forty minutes later, you are back inside. The whole job has taken you eleven hours.

On some shuttle flights a space laboratory is carried in the cargo bay. These astronauts are doing expeirments in the space laboratory.

Re-entry

Your stay in space is over. Now it is time for perhaps the most dangerous part of your mission – re-entry, or coming back to Earth.

Like most other jobs in space, there is a lot of preparation and checking to do first. The huge doors of the cargo bay must be closed. The rocket engines must be checked and made ready. The computers must be set for re-entry and checked with mission control. The shuttle must be turned so that it comes out of orbit tail first. You must all put on your special suits that will protect you during re-entry, and strap yourselves into your seats.

Three hours later, mission control says you can begin re-entry. The rocket engines fire and, in two minutes, they have gently pushed the shuttle out of its orbit. Then you turn the shuttle to go nose first, ready for re-entry.

As the shuttle re-enters Earth's atmosphere, it gets red-hot. There is a pink glow outside the cabin windows.

Twenty minutes go by, but nothing else seems to happen. Then suddenly you begin to feel heavier. The shuttle is slowing down. The air around it gets so hot it glows. Radio messages from mission control cannot get through.

Fifteen minutes later, the worst is over. The glow outside fades as the shuttle's speed drops. The shuttle glides in to land like an ordinary plane, twisting and turning to lose speed. You guide it towards the runway, lower the wheels, land and stop. You are safely back on Earth.

Wheels down, the shuttle orbiter comes in to land.

GLOSSARY, BOOKS TO READ

A glossary is a word list. This one explains unusual words that are used in this book.

Astronaut A person who travels in space. Russian astronauts are called cosmonauts.

Atmosphere The layer of air that surrounds Earth. Space begins beyond the atmosphere.

Cargo bay The area inside the shuttle orbiter where cargo is carried.

Comet Ball of frozen gas and dust in space. Comets travel in huge orbits that bring them in near the Sun from time to time.

Lunar module The part of the Apollo spacecraft that landed on the Moon.

Meteoroid A piece of rock that flies around in space.

Moon A small world that orbits a planet.

Orbit The path of a satellite, moon or planet as it travels round and round another object in space. The planets orbit the Sun and satellites orbit Earth.

Orbiter The part of the space shuttle that goes into orbit round Earth.

Planet A world that orbits the Sun. Earth is a planet.

Pressure The weight of air pressing down from above and around us.

Robot lander A machine, controlled by computers, that lands on the Moon or planets.

Rocket A very powerful engine that is used to launch spacecraft.

Rocket booster Extra rocket that is used during take off.

Mission control The people on the ground who are in charge of all space missions.

Satellite An automatic spacecraft that orbits Earth.

Spacecraft A machine that travels into space.

Space shuttle A type of spacecraft that is designed to be used again and again.

Space station A spacecraft that stays in orbit for long periods. Other spacecraft bring supplies and changes of crew.

Spacesuit A body-shaped, airtight bag that an astronaut must wear in space.

Star A huge ball of glowing gas in space. The Sun is our nearest star.

Weightlessness The feeling of not weighing anything at all that astronauts have in space.

BOOKS TO READ

Just Look At Space Exploration by Robin Kerrod, Macdonald Educational, 1983.

Just Look At Living in Space, by Robin Kerrod, Macdonald Educational, 1984.

Space Shuttle, Spacecraft, Satellites, Astronauts, all by N. S. Barrett, Franklin Watts, 1985.

Space by Tim Furniss, Franklin Watts/Aladdin Books, 1985.